Great Events

The
CORONATION
of QUEEN
ELIZABETH II

*Written and Illustrated
by Gillian Clements*

W
FRANKLIN WATTS
LONDON•SYDNEY

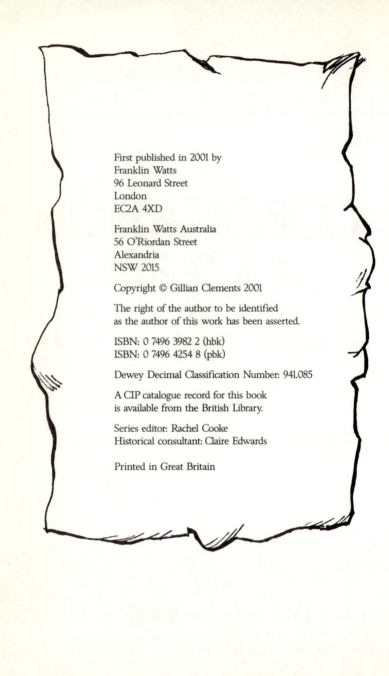

First published in 2001 by
Franklin Watts
96 Leonard Street
London
EC2A 4XD

Franklin Watts Australia
56 O'Riordan Street
Alexandria
NSW 2015

ISBN: 0 7496 3982 2 (hbk)
ISBN: 0 7496 4254 8 (pbk)

Dewey Decimal Classification Number: 941.085

A CIP catalogue record for this book
is available from the British Library.

Series editor: Rachel Cooke
Historical consultant: Claire Edwards

Printed in Great Britain

The CORONATION of QUEEN ELIZABETH II

WHOOSH! BANG!
The fireworks exploded in London's skies. Down below, thousands of excited people pressed into Piccadilly Circus. Someone shouted, "God Save the Queen". Twenty-seven year old Princess Elizabeth was crowned Queen that morning. It was Tuesday, 2nd June 1953.

Britain's Prime Minister, Winston Churchill, spoke into a large BBC microphone. "We have had a day which the oldest of us are proud to have lived to see, and which the youngest will remember all their lives." The street parties continued all night.

Elizabeth was born on 21st April 1926 – just eight years after the end of World War I. She was King George V's granddaughter. She called him "Grandpa England". The serious little girl and her young sister, Margaret, lived a quiet family life, walking dogs and riding ponies. Their home was the Royal Lodge by Windsor Castle. It was a happy time.

Then in 1936, old King George V died and everything changed for young Elizabeth.

Her uncle was next in line to the throne, but he had to abdicate later that year. Instead, Elizabeth's father became King George VI and her mother became Queen Elizabeth.

The family's quiet life was gone
forever. King George was a quiet,
simple man who stuttered when
he spoke. Being King was a
terrible strain – and just three
years later, the strain became far
greater. Britain was at war again.

BOOM! CRASH!! The screech of bombs falling and exploding tore the air. German troops had invaded countries in Europe. Now, in 1940, German warplanes blitzed and bombed their way across London, killing thousands.

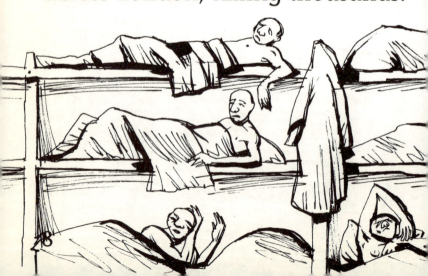

When bombs fell, Londoners scurried to the Underground. There were very few proper shelters. Above, in the East End, whole streets were turned to rubble and fire. Bodies lay in their flattened homes.

BAKER STREET

Then the Germans began to
bomb other British cities.
Thousands of city children were
evacuated – sent to live out of
harm's way in the country. The
Princesses Elizabeth and Margaret
were sent away from their London
home, Buckingham Palace, too.
Some nights they slept in the
dungeons under Windsor Castle!

Britain had to fight back, but it would be a long and difficult war. As the army and navy mobilised, a few hundred brave pilots fought the Germans in the skies above England. Many of them died, but they shot down even more enemy planes. The Battle of Britain saved the country from invasion.

Blood, toil tears and sweat!

Still the German bombing continued. The Prime Minister, Winston Churchill, had said there was nothing but "blood, toil, tears and sweat" ahead if Britain was to win the war.

The King and Queen shared their people's sorrow. When a bomb fell on Buckingham Palace the Queen wrote: "I'm glad we've been bombed. Now it makes me feel we can look the East End in the face."

The King began shooting practice in the Palace gardens. On her eighteenth birthday, Elizabeth joined the ATS (Auxiliary Territorial Service) as a trainee driver and mechanic. For the first time, the young princess mixed freely with people her own age. She had been educated at home, not in school with other children.

At last on the 8th May 1945,
the war in Europe ended.

Everyone celebrated.

"For He's a jolly good fellow,"
the happy crowd sang to the
King outside Buckingham Palace.
King George and his family stood
waving from the balcony.

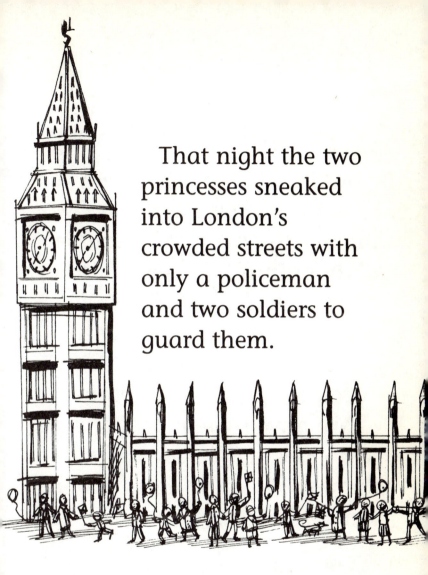

That night the two princesses sneaked into London's crowded streets with only a policeman and two soldiers to guard them.

"I pulled my uniform cap well down over my eyes," Elizabeth remembered.

But the street parties were soon over. After six years of war, the British were tired. Hundreds of thousands had been killed at home and abroad. Cities were bombed out, and the country was in debt. Food and other everyday goods were rationed.

"We have a great deal of work to do to win the peace as we won the war," said the new Labour Prime Minister, Clement Attlee.

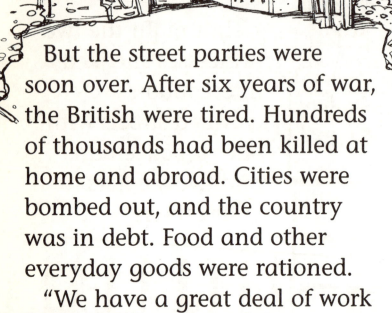

We have a great deal of work to do.

The Royal Family had its own work to do. But the King seemed old before his time. Years of worry had made him tired and ill.

It's unthinkable not to marry!

Elizabeth was young – nearly twenty. But, as heir to the throne, she was expected to marry. Not to do so was "unthinkable" said her old governess, Marion Crawford.

So the Princess made her choice, Prince Philip of Greece. He was a distant cousin who she had known as a child. He was in the Royal Navy.

In 1947 Princess Elizabeth and Prince Philip – now the Duke of Edinburgh – were married in Westminster Abbey.

It was a happy moment in a terrible year.

NOTICE
28 lb COKE
CUSTOMER
QUEUE HE

The winter of 1947 had been the worst in living memory. There was a shortage of bread and coal, so people were hungry and cold. On top of it all, the government had to raise people's taxes to help pay the country's debts.

19

The King looked at the world about him. "I do wish one could see a glimmer of a bright spot in world affairs," he said. "Never in the history of mankind have things looked gloomier than they do now."

Over the next few years, the King's health became worse.

Princess Elizabeth, meanwhile, had two children – Charles born in 1948 and Anne in 1950. Busy with her young family, she now also began to take over her father's royal duties.

In 1951 Elizabeth took the salute at Horse Guard's Parade. She looked a tiny figure as she rode to Whitehall.

In September, the king was found to have cancer, and surgeons removed a lung.

The country was suffering too. Rationing and long queues for food continued. Everything was in short supply. But some things lightened the gloom.

People were cheered by Elizabeth – their fairytale princess. She and her young children gave the country hope – surely things would soon change for the better.

PRINCESS VISIT! NEWS & PICTURES!

In fact, things were slowly improving. The 1951 Festival of Britain had been another ray of light in dark times.

Eight million people visited the festival on the south bank of the River Thames. It showed how exciting the future might be.

Now the shops began to fill with bright new things for the home. There was vinyl furniture, radiograms, washing machines, cookers and fridges. Most exciting of all was the television set!

The government was building new homes and new towns. In 1948 they had set up a National Health Service which gave free health care to everyone.

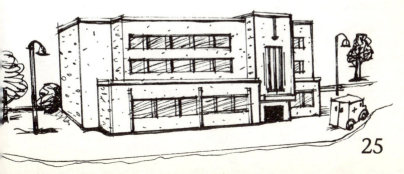

In the New Year of
1952, Elizabeth
and Philip set out
on a state tour to
Australia, visiting
Africa on the
way. King
George was too weak to go. So,
on the last day of January in the
wind and cold, King George
stood on the tarmac at London
airport. He was thin and pale,
as he waved goodbye to his
daughter and son-in-law.

In a few days the royal couple arrived in Kenya. They went on safari, staying at Treetops – a house nestling in the high branches of a huge old tree. The princess and prince had wonderful views of the wild animals below.

Back at Sandringham in
Norfolk, King George had eaten
dinner. He had enjoyed a good
day's shooting, but went to bed
early feeling tired. That night the
King died quietly in his sleep.

At dawn that day, Elizabeth and her companions had watched a huge fish eagle soar above Treetops. She didn't realise it at the time, but she was now Queen of Great Britain. It took several hours for the news of the King's death to reach the Royal Party. Prince Philip broke the tragic news to his wife.

The new Queen prepared to return to England immediately.

We will set a date for the Coronation

In London the government's Cabinet met to fix a date for the Coronation. Winston Churchill was once again Prime Minister, but he was a very old man. He wanted the Queen crowned before he retired. The date was set for 2nd June 1953.

At once there was excitement in the air. Life was getting better. The country was richer and rationing was nearly at an end. "This is a new Elizabethan Age," people said. "In Elizabeth I's day, England was young and exciting. Now Queen Elizabeth II will rule a new, modern country too."

People prepared for the big day – the greatest celebration since the war. They decorated their houses and shops in red, white and blue. It was like Christmas in midsummer. Town councils organised street parties for Coronation Day itself.

Queen Elizabeth's Coronation would be unique. TV cameras were set up at Buckingham Palace, and inside Westminster Abbey, where the coronation would take place. For the first time, everyone could see their monarch crowned! And millions around the world could watch too.

When June arrived, crowds of people flocked to London. Thousands camped out in the Mall. In the wind and rain, they lined the route all the way from the Palace to Westminster Abbey. Twenty-five million viewers sat down to watch television. In the streets, parties began.

Just before the Queen left Buckingham Palace, news spread through the waiting crowd. People clutched at newspapers.

"On 29th May at 11.30 a.m. New Zealander Edmund Hillary and Sherpa Tensing Norkay from Nepal, reached the 29,028 feet summit of Mount Everest," they read.

There were loud cheers.
It was a proud day. British and
Commonwealth teamwork had
made it possible for two men to
stand on the roof of the world.

Standing on the summit,
Sherpa Tensing held up a string
of flags, one for Nepal, one for
the United Nations, and a Union
Jack. It was the perfect news for
Britain and the Commonwealth
to hear on the day their new
Queen was crowned.

The Queen left Buckingham Palace for her Coronation in a beautiful gold coach, drawn by eight grey horses. It was a slow journey to Westminster. Kings, Queens and Prime Ministers – from every corner of the Earth – travelled behind.

Everyone found their place in the Abbey. The young Prince Charles watched from a balcony.

The Queen sat in St. Edward's golden throne, and the Coronation cermony began.

"Sirs, I here present unto you Queen Elizabeth, your undoubted Queen!" declared the Archbishop of Canterbury. The ceremony had changed little in a thousand years.

The Queen took her oath in a clear, high voice. She promised to rule with justice and mercy, and to protect the Church of England.

A choir began to sing. Out of sight of television cameras, the Archbishop anointed the kneeling Queen with oil. It was time for the crowning.

The Queen sat, with symbols of state – an orb, a sceptre, the rod of mercy, and a sapphire and ruby ring. Then the Archbishop placed St. Edward's crown on to the Queen's head.

"God save the Queen!" the Lords cried.

"God save the Queen!" echoed the congregation.

Church bells rang and trumpets sounded. Then "BOOM!" – at the Tower of London, cannons fired an ear-splitting salute.

The Archbishop blessed the Queen and paid homage, kissing her right hand. Then Prince Philip paid homage too. He kissed the Queen's left cheek.

"God save the Queen!" the congregation cried again. The words echoed in the Abbey.

"HOORAY!"

The crowd was wild with excitement when they saw the newly crowned Queen walk out of the Abbey into the rain. A cold wind lashed at the coach as it slowly returned to the Palace. Twenty-nine bands played, and thirteen thousand soldiers marched on the seven-mile route.

The crowds stayed outside
the Palace until nightfall.
The Palace balcony was
decorated scarlet and gold.
Just as the light faded, the
Queen stepped out again into
its floodlit glare.

"HURRAH!" The crowd cheered.
They tossed streamers and hats
into the air, and waved their flags.

The Queen turned on a switch,
and a river of light flashed like
lightning down the Mall. Soon
Nelson's Column, the West End
and City were bathed in light too.
Thirty thousand joyful Britons
surged into Piccadilly Circus, and
danced and sang until dawn.

All around Britain, people were
happy. The terrible war was over,
and they had a new, young
Queen. They thought life would
get better and better.

It was the dawn of a new day
and a new Elizabethan Age.

Timeline

1926   **26th April** Elizabeth is born.

1926   General Strike in May.

1933   Adolph Hitler becomes German Chancellor.

1936   **20th January** George V dies and his eldest son Edward VIII becomes King.
11th December Edward VIII abdicates in order to marry Wallis Simpson. They become the Duke and Duchess of Windsor.

1937   George VI is crowned.

1939   Germany invades Poland. Britain declares war on Germany. World War II begins.

1939   Women and children begin to be evacuated from London.

1940   King George VI and Queen Elizabeth I visit bombed out families in London.

1940   Butter and sugar are rationed.

1945   World War II ends.

1947 India gains independence from Britain marking the beginning of the end of the Empire.
Princess Elizabeth marries Philip Mountbatten, then Prince of Greece.

1948 The British Labour government sets up the National Health Service.
Princess Elizabeth gives birth to her first child, Prince Charles.

1950 Princess Anne is born.

1951 The Festival of Britain.

1952 King George VI dies in February.

1953 **29th May** Everest is conquered.
2nd June The Coronation of Elizabeth II is watched by 25 million viewers on black and white television.

1954 All rationing comes to an end.

1977 Queen Elizabeth's Silver Jubilee.
Peter Philips, the first of Queen Elizabeth II's grandchildren, is born to Princess Anne.

1997 Queen Elizabeth II and the Duke of Edinburgh celebrate their Golden Wedding anniversary in November.

Glossary

Abdicate When a King or Queen gives up their position.

Cabinet A special group of elected ministers that help govern a country.

Commonwealth The group of countries that used to be part of the British Empire and which still maintain some links. Elizabeth II is currently head of the Commonwealth.

Evacuation The movement of people from large cities, especially during World War II.

The Mall The road leading from Trafalgar Square to Buckingham Palace.

Mount Everest The highest mountain in the world, found in the Himalayas.

Rationing When the amount of food and goods you can buy is limited, or rationed, because of hard times.

Sandringham One of the royal family's country homes.

United Nations A large group of countries formed in 1945 to protect global justice and peace.